Old Roberton, Wiston Lamington and Coulte

by

Raymond Hood

The Lethgill, Littlegill or Ladygill (current name) area of Roberton (the name changes depending on which map you look at) takes its name from the burn of the same name which starts on Wildshaw Hill. In the upper part of this photograph from about 1925 can be seen Hillend Farm in the centre, with the cottages on either side which housed the ploughman and the shepherd (now holiday cottages). In the foreground, standing on the A73, on the extreme left are Hawthorn and Ivy cottages. Then there is Ladygill House, built about 1870 with two public rooms, six bedrooms, kitchen and two bathrooms plus its separate coach house. Then comes Ladygill Cottage adjacent to an open space which held a petrol pump and a wooden hut which doubled as a shop and pump attendant's office. Next to that is Clyde Cottage followed by another open space on which now stands a new bungalow. Beyond that there is Yarrow Cottages, built about 1910 to replace an earlier cluster of about seven farm labourers' cottages which had stood at right angles to the road. It is also recorded that in the early years of the hamlet there was a private school for girls located probably at Ladygill House; however, by 1901 the school had been moved to Lamington.

Text © Raymond Hood, 2016.
First published in the United Kingdom, 2016,
by Stenlake Publishing Ltd.
Telephone: 01290 551122
www.stenlake.co.uk

ISBN 9781840337501

Acknowledgements

I would like to thank Paul Archibald, Muir Jackson, Jill Kennedy, Stuart Russell, Margaret Currie, Ann Dobinson, Laura Maxwell-Stuart, Kenneth Tomory and Robert Tweedie for their help during the writing of this book. Also many thanks to my Sandra for her forbearance and encouragement.

Introduction

The four villages covered by this book have ancient origins, emerging from Iron and Bronze Age settlements and Roman roads and camps. It is from the sixteenth century however that we can trace their histories up to modern times. Flemish settlers and Normans were amongst the earlier people to arrive and they set about carving out little fiefdoms for themselves, their families and retainers. The village names reflect this Flemish influence, thus we have Robert's town, now Roberton, Wicces town, now Wiston, and Lamings town, now Lamington.

In the eighteenth century and into the nineteenth coach travel became the favoured mode of transport and also cattle were being driven south to the English markets. With the coming of the railways in the 1840s it became much easier to commute on business or pleasure and send goods to market. This brought wealthy industrialists into the area, buying large estates and building large country houses so they could indulge themselves with clean healthy air, farming interests, and country sports such as game shooting.

In the twentieth century the population dipped as increased mechanisation reduced the need for farming labour. Whilst some locals found employment in the large houses, even here servant numbers were being reduced and a number of the younger men did not return from the battlefields of the First World War. The 1920s saw houses being let out to holiday makers and others such as those suffering from tuberculosis and this continued into the 1940s. Also in the 1940s the War Department took over farms around Roberton for tank training purposes and troops and officers were billeted in some of the larger houses, which were also used to house evacuees. After the war the population declined again as it became much more expensive to run the larger estates and houses, some of which were demolished or left to rot. In the 1960s Dr Beeching axed the uneconomic railway lines and stations, and people had to depend on buses and private cars to get them to work. Thus, these rural villages remain small and somewhat remote but are nonetheless pleasant places to live.

ROBERTON AND DUNBROOKE HOUSE

Coming up Howgate Road from Townfoot, this view from about 1915 has hardly changed in the intervening years with the exception of tarred roads. On the left is Dunbrooke House, built in the 1830s and owned originally by a Dr James Dickson, a general practitioner and a surgeon at Glasgow's Victoria Infirmary. The house was extended about 1910 by John Finlay, a local joiner; the extension encroached onto the existing road creating a blind corner which is still referred to as Dunbrooke Corner although the house is now called Whitegables. To the immediate right of the house is Mill Cottage, which is built into the hillside with a lower basement which would have originally been the byre which held the livestock. Next to it, in the middle distance, the roof of the United Free manse can just be seen. To the right of the trees in the centre can be seen the old cornmill which is shown on a map of 1910 as being disused at that time, and beyond that Roberton Farm building can just be seen behind Millbrae House. Further right is The Cottage, a B-listed building dating from the sixteenth century.

Looking south-east down Howgate Road to the west end, the view in this 1920s photograph again has changed little in the intervening years. In the background the ridge of the United Free Church, built in 1843 and one of two churches in the village, shows above the roof of the U.F. church manse where the lady and her two boys stand at its gable end. On the right, is Rosebank with the lady in the garden, possibly Mrs Margaret Buchanan the postmistress at this time. Rosebank was the site of Roberton's first post office as until then there had been no official office. Across the road is Braehouse Cottage. The vacant space to the immediate right is now the site of a modern bungalow.

ROBERTON FROM LINN KNOWE

Taken from the Linn Knowe further up Howgate Road, this charming photograph dates from about 1910. It shows on the left outbuildings belonging to the mill and behind that the roof of Roberton farm. Adjacent to that is Millbrae House and alongside that the white painted gable of The Cottage. Above the trees is the parish church, built in 1905 on the site of an earlier church. To the right of the view there is someone at rest on a bench next to the bee hives in the garden of Mill Cottage. A hard working lady can be seen in the foreground laying out her washing on the grass slope.

A 1928 view from Howgate Road looking east into the Howtoun area of the village, showing the back of the mill buildings. No sign can be seen of the flume which brought the water along the back wall from the mill lade to the water wheel which was housed in the vertical opening that can see on the left. Above the mill outbuilding is the roof of Roberton Farm which was by then a private house and the roof and dormer of Millbrae House, built in 1882. In the centre of the photograph, to the left of the pedestrian, is The Cottage with Burnsands House beyond it. To the right can be seen the gable of the schoolhouse and in the shaded area the stone arch of the old single-arch bridge over Roberton Burn. On the far right Mill Cottage's back garden has a garden shed with a corrugated tin roof instead of the beehives seen in the earlier photograph.

Also taken in 1928, this view from the banks of the Roberton Burn looking east again shows the back of the mill buildings and its roof. The flume which took the water from the mill lade had run along the back wall but had gone by this time. On the other side of the rock outcrop on the left were a number of huts where crude curling stones were made about 1910 using stone bought in from Craighead Quarry near Crawfordjohn. Although no information survives it is probable that the power to grind the stones was provided by the millwheel. The last miller in the village was Thomas Jack in 1891. To the right is the slope of the Linn Knowe and the whitewashed back of Mill Cottage. From 1929 to the mid 1960s the mill, which had been gutted, was used as the village hall. It is now a private residence.

Taken from Dungavel Hill, overlooking the top of the cornmill and looking across Roberton Burn onto the slopes of the Linn Knowe, on the left is the six-bedroomed Ryefield House built about 1870. To the rear can be seen the roof of Woodside House and adjacent is the United Free church. To the right is the roof of the U.F. manse, now known as Longwood. On the other side of Howgate Road, down beside the burn can be seen Burnside Cottages. Above them, on the right of Howgate Road, is Braehouse and then Rowan cottages. Howgate Road follows the route of an old drovers' road.

Taken from the bank of Roberton Burn, this view shows the single-arched old bridge which replaced the ford which linked the west end and the Howtoun area of the village. The bridge, which may have been built in the sixteenth century, is wide enough to take a cart and would have eased access to the mill. It was the main bridge before the turnpike road bypassed the village; in living memory cars were driven across, although it is now a footbridge only. The mill itself shown on Ross's map of 1773 is of two and a half storey construction and was used mainly for grinding grain and produced curling stones in its later years. Above the mill wheel housing can be seen the remains of the water flume support. In 1929 the Douglas and Angus estates leased the mill to the village and it was converted into upper and lower halls, continuing in this use until the late 1960s.

Looking down from Howgate Road, this view looking across the burn to the Howtoun gives us a better view of the eastern half of the village. To the left we have Burnsands and on its right we see the gable and back of the old school with the two-storey schoolhouse (extended 1900) then, far right, the newer village school built in 1901. The village school was gifted by James Ferguson of Wiston Lodge who also gifted that one to Wiston. The school boasted several long serving teachers, the last one being Miss Christina Clarkson who held the post from 1926 to 1953. The red sandstone school is now in use as the village hall and has since been extended in recent years with the addition of a modern kitchen extension. Schoolchildren are now bused to Lamington and Biggar respectively. To the rear of the picture are the graveyard and the parish church, a B-listed building constructed in 1905 on the site of a much older church dating back to the thirteenth century. The graveyard is also the location of the village war memorial.

SCHOOL AND PARISH CHURCH, ROBERTON.

On the left behind the wooden shed is the back of Roberton schoolhouse which was extended about 1900. Just visible at the schoolhouse corner can be seen part of the last post office which was in use as a grocers and post office under the managements of variously Miss Jenny Bryans, Miss Colina Daly, Miss Brown and Mrs Thorburn. In 1961 Miss Jeannie McNeill took over and ran the post office and grocers until it finally closed in 1983. A better view of the red sandstone school can be seen here; it had about 33 pupils at any one time and closed in 1969 when it then became the village hall. Above the school behind the trees can be seen the roof of Marionton which was built about 1900 and replaced earlier cottages. To the left can be seen the parish (later East church) which closed down in 1929 and was renovated by the villagers in the late 1940s, continuing to be used for wedding and some church services. It is now a private residence.

With Tinto Hill in the background this angler is studying the water as he dexterously wields his fly rod hoping to tempt a trout with his cast. This photograph probably dates from about 1908, but it could have been taken yesterday. The sheep still graze the fields, the fishermen still fish. Renowned for their fighting ability, the trout in this area can reach up to 6lbs in weight and make it very worthwhile for an angler to take out a yearly license. The only building to be seen in this view is that of Tintoside Farm which can be seen on the lower slopes below Tinto Hill which reaches a height of 2,333 feet and is Lanarkshire's highest hill.

Flatbed harvest carts such as this were the mainstay of the farms around Wiston and district. They were not massive as the bigger the cart, the more horsepower required to pull it. Most farms could not afford large teams of horses or too many farmhands. Employed here to bring in corn or hay from the field, the horse is harnessed in normal working gear with a typical high peaked Scotch collar. In rough and hilly areas the carts tended to be smaller and have large diameter wheels with broad rims, firstly to cope with rough ground and secondly to give greater ease over soft ground. Another advantage was that wheels could be interchanged between carts in case of breakdowns. As can be seen here, the typical work wear even in hot weather was a waistcoat worn over a white shirt.

Belonging to Wiston Parish Church, this manse was built about 1840 and consisted of three reception rooms, six bedrooms and three bathrooms. It is located to the east of Wiston village, off Church Lane and across from the parish church, and was known as Duneaton Manse. This view from the bottom of Church Lane is dated about 1905. The minister at that time was a Rev. Harry Littledale Dick who was a keen golfer and held the course record for a number of years at nearby Roberton Golf Course. By the 1940s a Mrs Gibson was offering to rent apartments here with all modern conveniences. In the last 20 years it has been a nursing home, a holiday let and is now a private residence called Duneaton House.

POST OFFICE
WISTON

Wiston Post Office was located at the junction of Millrig Road and Church Lane, near to Mill Farm and would have been the social hub of the village. This view from around 1915 shows its sign on the gable. It provided postal services from a front room and supplied groceries, tea and tobacco amongst other items from the shed at the back of the cottage as well as a range of local postcards. Mrs Hamilton was the sub-postmistress from 1898 to about 1915. As can be seen, it was housed in a substantial little cottage built from coursed whinstone rubble with small windows and a slated roof. Over the years it has seen changes, the gable now has two narrow windows and an inset George V red post box. To the rear the lean-to shed has been replaced by a modern conservatory and the exposed stonework of the building is now whitewashed and it goes by the name of West Cottage.

In this photograph of the post office the back of the cottage is shown from a slightly different viewpoint. As with most village shops of the period the shop stocked basic groceries, newspapers, tea, sweets, pins and needles and possibly spirits and tobacco from a back room plus whatever Marion Hamilton the shop owner could squeeze in. The shop is in the corrugated tin shed which has been built onto the back of the cottage. The horse is harnessed in normal working harness with the exception of the English-style collar. The large wheels on the cart would have been equally at home carrying up to seven and a half hundredweights of manure across a rough field as they were on the road.

Wiston, unlike Roberton, only had one church. This was built in Gothic style about 1840 and had seating for 400 people. Like the manse it was situated at the top of Church Lane on a hill overlooking the Garf Water. Wiston Church contains some fine Arts and Crafts-inspired stained glass windows made by Stephen Adam and Son, a Glasgow firm. It is possible that the group of people seen here in this 1910 postcard, published by Mrs Hamilton of the post office, include the Rev. Littledale Dick and his wife. The graveyard surrounds the church and enclosing the graveyard is a six-foot-high raised embankment. The church also has stained glass windows in memory of villagers who died in the First World War. Closed down in 1986 and sold in 1987, the church is now a private residence.

Wiston School was built about 1840, just off Millrig Road, due to the generosity of James Ferguson of nearby Wiston Lodge. This view from 1908 shows the schoolhouse to the left; take note of the gate set into the garden wall which would give the schoolmaster of the time, James Waddell, access to the small school sitting alongside. The school was built to cater for about thirty pupils and they would have varied in ages up to seventeen. It was administered by the local school board at this time. The old school was demolished in 2012 and the pupils decanted to Tinto School while a new school of two classrooms, staff rooms, kitchen, toilets and dining-cum-gym hall was built in its place. The schoolhouse is now a private residence.

Looking north down Millrig Road from near Marchlands Farm, Wiston Cornmill's rubble-built, two-and-a-half-storey L-plan building can be seen to the immediate left of the picture. Built possibly in the early 1700s and shown on Forrest's map of 1813, it was used to grind the corn and oats grown locally. This postcard dating from about 1913 shows a small cart loaded with hay or oats at the road junction, maybe going to the farm for threshing. The mill was included in a for sale notice of 1938 as part of the Wiston Estate. The last miller here was a William Clarkson in the 1940s and it had been in his family for at least two generations. Fallen into disuse by 1960 it was stripped of all its machinery in 1976 and was used as a store by Mill Farm for a number of years. Nowadays it is a private house. Across the road, in the middle of the picture, a part of the front and gable of the shop and post office can be seen; immediately below are the farm outbuildings and Mill Farm to the far right. Today all the buildings are private homes with the exception of the outbuildings which are now stables for Mill Farm.

This view looks roughly southwest down Millrig Road to Marchlands Farm, which was once owned by Mr Robert McCosh of Hardington House. On the right can be seen the front of Wiston Mill and the mill house. Out of picture to the left is Mill Farm and in the field beside the farmer and his family are a number of small hayricks. Taken in July or August, this 1920s' postcard shows the farmer and his wife and daughter chatting to a neighbour on the roadside. The hayricks wait for the rick-lifter cart, a small-wheeled cart with a tilting back which was backed into position against the rick. Ropes were put around the rick and a handle at one side of the cart was turned, tightening the ropes and dragging the rick onto the cart. The cart then took them to their final location where they were either built into one large haystack and thatched and roped down, or put into a hay barn. Of course today they would have been baled and wrapped shortly after being harvested.

Built in the 1850s by the merchant James Ferguson as a hunting lodge, Wiston Lodge is set in an estate of around 52 acres. The Ferguson family were involved in coal mining – James owned Auchenheath Colliery near Lesmahagow – and the sugar industries. The lodge was built in Scots Baronial style and contained a hall, five public rooms, seven bedrooms and ample bathrooms, kitchen and servants' quarters and other accommodation. It was extended in the late nineteenth century and again in 1913 with the addition of a small concert hall, which is now closed off awaiting repair. The estate had extensive greenhouses, garage accommodation for five cars, and houses for a chauffeur, two gardeners, and a forester. Note the unique tower with its accompanying octagonal tower alongside, one of only two similar structures known in Scotland. In 1945 the building was bought by the YMCA as a holiday and conference centre until its sale to the Wiston Trust in 2009. A B-listed building, it has hardly changed and its interiors are of great importance. At present it is now a venue for team building activities, has close links with colleges and caters for visits from school groups. The estate was extensively laid out, with all its tracks lined with beech trees. Many of the outbuildings are in a ruinous state at present but the intention is to repair and bring them back into use.

Looking northwest from the Abington to Lanark road (now the A702) towards Tinto Hill, Wiston Parish Church can be seen in the trees to the left. Immediately to the right is the church manse with the slope of Tinto Hill behind. Alongside the road in the foreground, Castledykes Smithy is on the right with its outbuildings to the rear. Not a lot is known about this smithy but it is shown as such in maps from 1856 up until 1926. It would have been ideally placed for looking after the shoeing of the carriage horses at nearby Chester Hall in the early 1800s when the coaching trade was at its peak, and also the plough horses of the nearby farms. The last blacksmith known here was a John Smith in the late 1920s and this photograph dates from then. Today the cottage houses an antiques centre.

Chester Hall, Wiston

Chester Hall lies on the outskirts of Wiston alongside the A702. It is Georgian in style and was probably built as an overnight stop for coaching traffic in the 1700s, with ample room for stabling coach horses in the adjoining buildings and allowing a changeover of the teams. In the 1840s it rivalled Roberton's inn for similar services and was an alternative stop for thirsty travellers. The plain frontage that can be seen here, built of coursed whinstone with decorative quoins, understates its importance. Out of picture to the left is a coach house with two arched doorways capable of accommodating large coaches. This view probably dates from about 1900 or slightly earlier as a sign painted on the roof parapet can just be made out; in recent memory there was also a painted sign on the lintel over the front door saying Chesterhall Inn. To the rear there is a large enclosed stable yard incorporating servants' cottages on its left-hand side and stables to the right. The house and farm was occupied in 1868 by a R. Muirhead and in 1894 by an Alexander Williamson. In 1896 Mr Williamson was made bankrupt and a 'displenishment' sale was held. A further for-sale notice of 1914 stated that the farm steadings were in good condition and were part of Wiston Estate. In 1935 a roadman from Wiston Cottages was one of two roadmen knocked down on the road at Chester Hall. George Little was killed instantaneously, whereas his companion was only bruised and able to walk home. Today the house has lost its picket fence. It is occasionally let and the remainder of the steading is incorporated into farming use.

This photograph appeared on a postcard dated 1907 and shows Hardington House, built in 1720. It is thought that the house was extended in Victorian times by the addition of the wings that can be seen on either side of the older house. The house was described in 1921 as having an entrance hall, dining room, drawing room, six principal bed and dressing rooms, two bathrooms and ample servant's quarters. The gardens and grounds included tennis courts, four cottages and a home farm; it is now a B-listed building as is its associated stable range with its clock tower. Sitting in its own large estate it lies between the Lanark and the Biggar roads near to Lamington. It would seem to have been built for an offshoot of the Baillie family of Lamington. In 1940 a Mr Robert McCosh was resident here and was recorded as attending the funeral of the late Lord Lamington at his estate. The estate was known for good low ground shooting and up to 60 to 70 brace of grouse in a good season. Recent work on the roof revealed that the roof spars were sawn on one face only, showing that when built local timber from the estate was used. At present a Mr Robin McCosh is the owner.

The Parsonage was built by Alexander Baillie-Cochrane about 1860, to house the minister of nearby Holy Trinity Chapel. It was designed by John Henderson who had designed the chapel in 1857. The house was one of a number of buildings which replaced older bothies that had stretched along the old roadside. Baillie-Cochrane had the old road to Coulter and Biggar redirected to afford more privacy to Lamington House and had the bothies demolished. In 1926, when this photograph was taken, its occupant would have been Mr James McElhose, the owner of a Glasgow printing firm. The open porch with stone pillars has the initials 'ABC' inscribed on one pillar, standing for Anabella Baillie-Cochrane. The building still retains most of its original features but has had a few later features added. In the twentieth century it was used as the Opportunity Holiday House before being converted in 1996 to a residential care home for the Autistic Society, now known as Clannalba House.

This late-nineteenth-century cottage, seen here in the 1930s, was known as the 'Pump House'. The pump which gave the cottage its name was housed under the pyramidal tiled roof in the foreground. At one time it was the custom of the occupant to come out at one minute past midnight on New Year's Eve and be the first to use the pump. Although the housing is still in place the pump has been stripped out and a drain cover is now all that can be seen. All of the buildings in the village are marked in some way with the initials of Anabella Baillie-Cochrane, usually in a panel but sometimes chiselled into a pillar or a corner stone or quoin with a date nearby. Currently known as Belleview, this would have been one of the earlier cottages to be erected in this model village which was built by Lord Lamington partly as a mark of his prestige and partly to move tenants out of the policies of Lamington House.

"The Cottage" and School House, Lamington.

The schoolmaster's cottage shown on the left is a B-listed building and was built in the mid 1800s as part of the planned Lamington estate. It is a two-storey three-bedroom cottage with a rear extension and Tudor-style chimneys. In 1926, when this photograph was taken, this was the home of James Patterson, the local schoolmaster. Out of picture on the left was the school. This was taken over by the local school board in 1912 but then went into decline. To the right is Jubilee Cottage, built in 1887 as a dower house for the dowager 1st Lady Lamington. At some point in time the cottage was called Drumgeith and more recently the name changed to Penryhn Cottage. Modern changes have been made to Jubilee Cottage with an extension to its rear and the front doorway built up, a window installed in its place and the door relocated. In 1955 both the cottages shown were made listed buildings but the school, also listed, was later de-listed and this led to its demolition in 2013. The village now has a new school which opened in June 2014 on the site of the previous one.

The A-listed Lamington Tower was probably built in the sixteenth century. It is thought to have been a simple keep or tower house built by the Jardine family of Hardington and Wandell and later extended. The ruins of the tower stand on a gravel mound above the level haugh of the Clyde, near to Hardington House. The ruinous walls now stand about three to four metres high and the south wall has a date stone of 1859 with the initials E.B. (possibly commemorating a member of the Baillie family) set into the wall. In the adjacent field was the remains of a fragmented turret from the building, dating from 1780 when the building was blown up by the factor. Mary, Queen of Scots, is reported as visiting the tower in 1565. The tower was occupied until 1750 but was robbed for its stone by the estate factor in 1780. This photograph dates from the 1920s as by the 1950s, when first listed, the height was given as three to four metres and the stonework of the tower was stabilised to stop further damage.

This view of the west end of Lamington Parish Church would have been taken in the 1920s from a position in front of the old school. It is the only church in the village although there is also a chapel. The church was built about 1771. It incorporates in its north wall a Norman arched doorway of the original twelfth century church which had been dedicated to St Ninian. The church was renovated in 1828 and again about 1880. It is said that in February 1789 a visit by Burns led to him complaining about the lack of heating and supposedly inscribing on a window the following lines, 'As cauld a wind as ever blew, A cauld kirk and in't but few'. On the east side of the Norman doorway can be seen the iron staple which once held the 'jougs' to which wrongdoers were once shackled. About 1922 a stone tablet listing the names of the local men who died in the First World War was incorporated into the doorway. No longer used for worship, the nearest churches are in Abington, Symington and Biggar. The church and chapel, which is at the east end of the village alongside the main road but within the grounds of Lamington House, are both now listed buildings.

Lamington House was built for Alexander Baillie-Cochrane, a grandson of the Earl of Dundonald. Baillie-Cochrane was a Conservative MP for St Pancras from 1896 to 1890. Originally Alexander Cochrane, he was aide to Lord Salisbury, the Prime Minister in 1885/86. When he inherited the Baillie family estate of Lamington in 1838 he changed his name to Baillie-Cochrane, and about 1844 he set about enlarging an existing shooting lodge to form Lamington House. The house was built in the style of a modern Elizabethan mansion. It was about this time that he also caused the main road to be redirected to give the house more privacy and set about building the model village that exists today, demolishing the older bothies that had lined the old road. In October 1876 it was the venue for a royal visit by Prince Leopold, Queen Victoria's son. A ball was held in Prince Leopold's honour with over 200 guests including Lord and Lady Home of Douglas, Sir Edward Colebrooke and the Countess of Breadalbane. In 1880 he was created the 1st Lord Lamington. Succeeded by his son Charles in 1890, who married the granddaughter of Lord Newlands, Charles became Governor of Queensland, Australia, and later Governor of Bombay. In 1936 he was a captain in the Royal Company of Archers of Scotland, the King's ceremonial bodyguards. Charles died of a heart attack in 1940 and was buried in the Holy Trinity Chapel which his father had built on the estate. Victor Baillie-Cochrane became the 3rd Lord Lamington but only held the title for eleven years, dying in 1951 and leaving no heir so the title became extinct. From 1939 to 1942 the house was used as accommodation for evacuated children under the care of a Mrs Thompson who was Matron. In the 1960s it was demolished, leaving no trace.

Like other estate owners in the area, such as Lord Home of Douglas and Sir Edward Colebrooke at Abington, the 1st Lord Lamington had suitable parts of his land laid out for gentle recreation. In nearby Lamington Glen he had graded paths laid out with rustic bridges and a number of clearings at suitable intervals. In these clearings were heather thatched huts, or fog houses as they were known locally. The sender of this postcard referred to the hut shown as the 'lover's hut'. The pool seen here was known as Lord Lamington's Pool and was located on the Lamington Burn. It was used by the lord, his family and guest's, as a swimming pool, and as can be seen he had a heather thatched dressing hut built as a changing room. Also to aid access to the pool he had the wooden steps constructed and fixed in place. This photograph possibly shows Lord Lamington himself. Today the glen is part of Baitlaws Estate and the paths can still be traced in sections although the huts have gone.

Baitlaws House is thought to have been built for the farm manager of Lamington Estate in the 1840s. In the 1851 census an Alexander Denholm, farmer, is listed as residing here with his wife and three daughters. The household also consisted of three house servants, three farm servants and one shepherd. The farm consisted of about 88 acres at this time and would have been part of the larger Lamington Estate. In 1857 Alexander Denholm was a well-known and respected judge of the Blackface breed of sheep, judging at a number of shows. In the 1940s Baitlaws passed to the Lesley-Melville family who were related to Lord Lamington, Lady Melville being a sister of the 2nd Lord Lamington and married to Henry Dundas, 5th Viscount Melville and Baron Dundas. In the late 1950s the young Prince Carl Gustav of Sweden, who had been educated at Eton with the son of the Lesley-Melville family, used to come and stay at Baitlaws over the summer months. Locals recall that he helped with the harvesting on the estate farm. In the 1970s it was bought by its present owners, the Maxwell Stuart family.

Looking towards Townfoot, this photograph from the 1920s shows the post office van parked next to Roselea Cottage, now just called The Cottage. On the left the ground beyond the trees has been cleared and is now the village bowling green and playground. Today most of the cottages are listed buildings and have hardly changed since they were built, but there are now no trees lining the street.

The Post Office, Lamington.

A 1905 postcard showing Lamington Post Office, built in the mid-nineteenth century. Unlike other buildings in the village, it and the neighbouring shop are built out of blonde coloured sandstone. In 1905 the post mistress was Elizabeth Forrest, followed in 1908 by a James Pettigrew. The shop next door was run by a Janet Dempster and later by a Miss McKendrick; between them they would have covered stamps, newspapers, stationery, groceries, and household necessities. The post office and the shop closed in the 1970 and are now private residencies.

This 1931 view of Coulter was taken looking north towards the Birthwood Road junction from a position in front of Coulter Mill. On the far left, parked at the side of the road, is an early motorbike, and the car is approaching the junction. The cottage in the background is one of a line of weaver's cottages. The cottage in the centre is that of the smiddy of William Haddon, which was in the process of evolving into a garage as well. There have been changes since this photograph was taken; over the years, as traffic accidents occurred regularly with trucks demolishing the wall on the left, so the road was levelled and re-aligned, taking away the end weaver's cottage and improving the road junction.

This photograph looking east from a field to the south of the main road gives a better view of Coulter Mill to the right. Built in the nineteenth century, it is thought to have been the second mill to have existed in Coulter. It is a typical two-and-a-half storey mill building and had a mill wheel which took its power from the mill lade. The mill lade started at Craigend Weir about one mile further up Coulter Water and would then be returned to Coulter Water. Like other mills it would have processed locally grown grain and turned it into flour or oats as required. The miller when this photo was taken about 1910 was Robert B. Forrest. In the centre of the photograph we see part of the smithy and the cottage on the right which housed the shop of Frank Anderson. Behind the smithy is the roof of the weavers' cottages. In the 1820s weaving was the best paying employment for rural workers and typically the loom would be in one room and the family would live in the other. The mill is now a restaurant and the cottages private residences.

Craig Quarry was located on the lower slopes of Shaw Hill, about a mile up the Birthwood Road at Craigend, near to Coulter Craigs. It lies alongside the single-arched bridge which spanned Coulter Water. In the immediate foreground to the right we can see the mill lade which started at Craigend Weir just above the bridge. The weir raised the level of the watercourse by about three feet and the sluice gate could be opened or closed as needed. The quarry opened in the early nineteenth century and would have supplied most of the whinstone needed to build the houses of the village. The quarry would also have supplied rock needed for building Coulter Reservoir. In the 1990s a large uprooted tree badly damaged the mill lade and that, with the broken millwheel, closed the restored mill for good. Since then the bridge has had its parapet walls removed and they have been replaced by simple iron railings.

Coulter Library near Biggar.

A 1920s view of Coulter Library and Reading Room. It was first proposed in 1838 and R. G. Baillie esquire of Coulter Allers gifted the site. However, it was not until 4 August 1888 that the foundation stone was laid. Alexander Kay of nearby Cornhill House covered the cost of the building. In 1905 a Mathew Lamb was the parish librarian and was listed as running the post office as well; on the top right of the wall of the adjoining caretaker's cottage can be seen a post office sign. By 1910 the librarian was a Walter Douglas and Mr Lamb had left, taking the post office business with him. The library contained 1,800 volumes by 1921. It sits just across the road from Coulter Mill and was closed in 1967, its place now taken by the travelling library van.

CORNHILL HOUSE, BIGGAR.

Cornhill House was extended, as shown here, about 1868 by William Leiper, architect for a Mr Kay. Leiper was noted for his design of a number of large buildings and churches throughout the west of Scotland, his most famous design being the Templeton Carpet Factory in Glasgow. Out of picture on the left is a plainer Georgian wing. Cornhill House resembles a French chateau in style and was influenced by Leiper's early studies in France. The interior also reflected this French influence. In 1900 the house was acquired by a Mr James Young, a well-known Glasgow contractor. With the exception of a large modern glazed conservatory which overlooks the Clyde the exterior of the building has hardly changed since this photograph was taken about 1920. For a period of about 30 years the house was used by Lanark County Council as a care home for the elderly, but it is now a hotel.

THE LOUNGE, CORNHILL HOUSE.

The lounge of Cornhill House. As an interior designer Leiper was very versatile, designing the interior of the Russian royal yacht *Livadia*. Today this lounge is the hotel dining room but still retains the original style and fireplace.

Coulter Main Street, about 1900, looking northeast from a field near to the mill. The building nearest is that of William Gordon, joiner. Just beyond that we have the mill itself. Parked on the street in front of the buildings, the cart with the large barrel was probably a water cart for taking water around the village houses, possibly awaiting repair. A cart can be seen on Coulter Bridge and beyond that another. The mill itself was restored by volunteers to full working order about 25 years ago but a combination of extreme temperatures and severe frost froze the mill lade and the strain broke up the wheel and caused irreparable damage. In 1990 the mill became a hotel and the damaged wheel can now be seen to the rear of the hotel set in a replica section of the mill lade.

Post Office Coulter.

This was Coulter's second post office which was located on the Biggar road, just over the old Coulter Bridge. In 1910 when this photograph was taken the postmaster was a Mathew Lamb and any mail came via Biggar. On the far right can be seen the roofs of the cottages which parallel the Coulter Water. There were two postal deliveries and as with other villages the post office was incorporated within a home and run by its owner. A message on the reverse of this postcard refers to the rails which can be seen on the road on the left-hand side. These were associated with the building of Coulter Reservoir and the track ran from Coulter to Causwayhead and up Birthwood Road until it reached the railhead at the dam. Today the building is a private house known as Tiree and the nearest post office is in Biggar.

COULTER HOUSE.

Coulter House is located just to the east of the A702 as the road leaves the village heading for Biggar. Within sight of the road, it is approached via a gated lodge entrance. It was built around the core of earlier buildings possibly dating back to the sixteenth century. The house comprises a central Georgian building, built in 1838, with two plainer wings. In 1920 Baron Ferrier, the then owner, had the building on the left connected with the main building. About the same time a house was built on the other side of the main road for the nanny and this later housed Coulter Post Office. Set in a small 34-acre estate, Coulter House boasts a magnificent avenue of deciduous trees to the rear. Deceptive in appearance, it appears that even the wing to the east had five bedrooms. Recently a wheelchair-friendly house has been built to the rear for the Bell family who have owned Coulter House for the last twenty years.

Coulter Mains was recorded as a sixteenth-century tower house owned by the Brown family until 1753, by which time it was in ruinous condition. It was acquired in 1817 by a David Sim whose son Adam became a noted antiquary. In 1838 the Sim family commissioned William Spence, a Glasgow architect, to design and build a new house around the ruin of the older one. This was built in the Elizabethan Gothic style and it incorporated ornate ceilings, plasterwork and wood panelling, as well as former farm buildings. Spence was involved at the nearby Lamington Estate and elements of his design were influenced by it. In 1918 it was described as having five public rooms, nine bedrooms, three dressing rooms, a bathroom and other accommodation, with an excellent water supply. Outside were offices, a large coach house or garage, a coachman's house and stabling. This early photograph would have been taken about 1920. At present it is owned by Sir Graeme Davies, a former vice chancellor of Glasgow University. A one-acre walled garden with 100-year-old Rhododendron bushes has been restored by them in recent years and the resulting garden is now opened to the public once a year.

Taken in the 1920s, this photograph of Coulter Station shows the station building and the stationmaster's house on the left. The stationmaster at this time was a William McCrae. As can be seen, the main line was a single track with a siding and a road crossing at the end of the platform. The station was opened by the Caledonian Railway about 1860 and was better known for its beef cattle traffic than passenger traffic. When built, the station encroached into the Coulter motte. The line was closed to passengers in June of 1950 and to goods in June 1966; the station is long gone and only the stationmaster's house remains as a private dwelling.

A photograph from about 1905, showing the construction of Coulter Reservoir at the top of the Coulter Water in the Coulter Fells. The narrow-gauge track from Coulter is in the foreground and it was extended as the embankment grew in length. In the middle distance two locomotives are at the top of the embankment, one with tipper trucks possibly full of puddled clay to line the reservoir. The dam was built by the firm of Sir Robert McAlpine, and is of earthen-embankment construction stretching across the valley. The temporary village was called Waterhead and consisted of a school, a mission hall, canteen, reading room, grocery and workers' barracks. The sale of beer and spirits to the navies was strictly licensed. The 54-acre reservoir was built to supply water to Motherwell originally, but today supplies Biggar, Coulter and parts of Carnwath. Note the bicycle at the side of the track, maybe the quickest way to send instructions to the railhead.

WATER WORKS, COULTER

A further view of the reservoir works, this one taken looking down from the flanks of Snowgill Hill. This view shows the top of the embankment and the extended rail line. To the left of the photograph can be seen the draw-off tower surrounded by scaffolding. The tower housed the valves which feed water to the purification plant and then into the system. From behind the tower and crossing from the left to the right can be seen the internal face of the dam. This face would have been a thick layer of puddled clay with a facing of cement-pointed rocks to prevent leaks. Above that can be seen the track crossing the flanks of Knockhill on its way to the end of the reservoir. When the reservoir is filled it holds approximately 2.2 million litres of water.

In the early twentieth century most rural cottages such as this one at Chapelhill near Coulter would have been heather thatched. It was a free material, easily come by, light in weight and long lasting when laid properly. As can be seen, access was a problem here with only a footpath and a footbridge leading to the cottage. In a remote area such as this a keeper or shepherd had to be a jack of all trades and be able to carry out running repairs. Note the steep pitch of the roof which allowed an extra two rooms in the attic with access by a ladder from below. Alongside to the right are the byre and storage shed.

Coulter Parish Church dates from the seventeenth century and the current building, dating from 1721, incorporates part of one from 1655. The church was located on the Broughton road near to the village, in a corner of the Coulter Estate. The church was renovated in 1818 and again in 1874 at a cost of over £900. It was not the only church in the village as in 1843 the United Free church had a presence also. At the time of this 1921 photograph the parish minister was the Rev. John Cowan Hamilton and the U.F. church was vacant. As was customary each of the large houses would have its own pew in a prominent position in relation to the pulpit. There is a private path to the rear of the church leading to Coulter House. The graveyard contains some fine early seventeenth-century gravestones. There is also a memorial to a James Gillray who died in 1815 and was a political satirist and caricaturist of the Georgian and Napoleonic period. A Covenanting minister, Antony Murray, who hid out in the Coulter Fells before his capture and execution, also has a memorial in the churchyard. Coulter's war memorial is built into the churchyard wall. Today the church is a private residence with the nearest place of worship in Biggar.